"The role we play in life changes,
with time and circumstances,
and while we don't always have control, over the role we are placed in,
we do have control, over the way
we play that role."

Mike Siver 2001 ©

What Role Did I Play
Volume II
Life Skills for Discussion

Mike Siver

m.a.c. / c.d.v.c. / b.c.b.c.
Master Addictions Counselor
Certified Domestic Violence Counselor
Board Certified Biblical Counselor

Foreword/Edited by: Ken Hayes, CLC, CNHP

authorHOUSE®

AuthorHouse™
1663 Liberty Drive
Bloomington, IN 47403
www.authorhouse.com
Phone: 1-800-839-8640

First published by AuthorHouse   3/17/2011

ISBN: 978-1-4567-0053-9 (sc)
ISBN: 978-1-4567-0052-2 (e)
ISBN: 978-1-4567-0054-6 (hc)

Library of Congress Control Number: 2011900446

Printed in the United States of America

Introduction

These stories are from a larger book titled, **"What Role Did I Play"**.
"What Role Did I Play" was written after many years of counseling, Individual youth, teens, families and family groups.

The question continued to come up about the role the adults played, In the child, youth or teens upbringing.
By the end of a series of sessions, most participants would have the knowledge, To ask, **what role** am I playing in the current situation?
What are the possible consequences?

These short stories will generate a lot of conversation, and discussion, within families and groups, as well as provide participants, with a little knowledge of life skills and **What Role they are playing in their life.**

Mike Siver, msmf, mac, ccdvc, cbc
Performance Coach

Foreword:

In **"What Role Did I Play"**, Mike explains
The life skills necessary, for adults and children,
To succeed in life.
How our actions, reactions, and words,
Play a critical role, in our development as
Successful adults.
These stories are a platform, are easy to learn
and used as tools, in learning how to interact
with everyone, in the many different roles
we play throughout our lives.
The following stories will inspire healthy
discussion and debate in your family,
as they have in mine.

Ken Hayes,
Christian Life Coach
Certified Natural Health Professional

Contents

The Sponge ©
June 6/1998

For Tuck, Haans, Mark, C.J., James, & David

Father and Stepfather

When we are born we are like a new sponge, we are clean and empty.
There is neither love nor hate. A baby, like the sponge, has to stay in and
absorb whatever is in the atmosphere it is living.
If the atmosphere is full of love, support, kindness, honesty, fair play,
ethical thinking, accepting of others, then this is what we will absorb.
If the atmosphere is full of hate, distrust, lying, drugs or alcohol, bigotry,
racism, and all for ME, then this is what we will absorb.

Whatever atmosphere (community or family) we grow up in, we
(like the sponge) will keep absorbing until we are full.
Then whatever we are full of will start to flow back out.
If that is love, kindness, honesty, fair play, ethical thinking and accepting
of others, then that is what you will give back to those around you in the
community and family. If you fill up on hate, distrust, lying, drugs or
alcohol, bigotry, and racism then that is what you will give back to those
around you
in the community and family.

Unlike the sponge, or new baby, as we get older we have a choice of what
we want to absorb. If you are in an unhealthy community or family it
may be very hard to change, because it will make you different, and to be
different you have to be very strong.
**"The greatest power we have as human is
to make a choice."**

If a person starts to think, "What role am I playing in my life?" that person
decides to change, they may need some help. This can come in many
forms. It could be moving out of the unhealthy atmosphere, maybe going
to jail, going to a rehabilitation, behavior program, individual or family
counseling, or finding religion. This could be related to wringing out the
sponge.

If the sponge is put in a clean bowl of water, it will start to become clean.

As we know, at first the clean water will become dirty and may have to be changed several times. A person full of hate, distrust, lying, drugs or alcohol, bigotry, and racism will try and make the new environment like the one they left, because that is all they know. This is where the demand for consistent support is the strongest.

Like the sponge, depending on how long and how unhealthy the atmosphere was, the person may have to make several attempts to become clean or change the behavior. Changing the atmosphere is not enough, there must be love and understanding combined with a lot of education.

The education isn't just for the individual, but may have to involve the family and community. Everyone involved with that person must have the same knowledge to provide the support needed. With this education, mixed with love and care, the person will live through this, and with time, be able to break the mold and take on the responsibility of a person who will one day be proud of "What role they are playing", and one day bring a baby into the world...

Teach our Children

If we teach our children
by example, then we have
**only ourselves to blame for
what they become!**
As parents, do we really accept responsibility,
for the actions of our children?
or do we say, "We taught them right from wrong."
and "They should have known better."

As we think about the role we play, as parents in our children's lives, what comes to mind?

Some say, "I want them to have more than I did as I grew up." or "I don't want them to be treated the way I was."

Those are both great thoughts and most of us have similar ones, while some of us will have a couple more; also good and relative to that parent.

My question is, "Do those thoughts have anything to do with your child being held accountable and responsible for their actions?"

We are, as parents, responsible for the actions of our children until they are considered legal adults.

It seems we are always ready to take responsibility and credit when our children do well. If they are "A" students, a basketball star, president of the student body, or any number of positive accomplishments. We do not tell the parent who tells us, "You have done a great job with your child... You must be so proud."

We do not say, "We had nothing to do with it. It's their fault. We taught them right from wrong."

When our children get into trouble, the same parent comes and says, "You have to watch your child more." It's then you say, "It's not our fault, we taught them right from wrong. They should have known better. We're doing the best we can." But this is where we do not want to take responsibility.

The role we play as parents, does not stop and start when it suits us.

The Little Boy and the Old Man

Said the *little boy*, "Sometimes I drop my spoon"
Said the little *old man*, "I do that too"
The *little boy* whispered, "I wet my pants"
"I do that too", laughed the little *old man*
Said the *little boy*, "I often cry"
The *old man* nodded, "So do I"
"But worst of all" said the boy, "It seems Grownups
Don't pay attention to me"
And he felt the warmth of a wrinkled old hand.
"I know what you mean," Said the little *old man*.

From A Light in the Attic

We give all the attention needed, to support them growing up.
If our young children drop their spoon, or anything else, we pick it up for them, or allow them time to do it, so they feel good about themselves.
If our young children wet their pants, we know they do not do it on purpose, so, without wanting to embarrass them, we let, or help them change clothes, and do not make a scene about it.

If our young children start to cry, we ask why, and work very hard to understand. We also reassure our children, it is okay to cry, and those who love them will hold their hand until they feel better.

If our young child is looking lonely, we will sit with them, and make sure, they are included more with the family activities until they stop feeling like no one is paying attention to them.

Why is it, after being given all the support, and attention, we need as children, we treat those who gave us that support with such abandon?
Why is it, that after being made to feel good when we were down, being

picked up after when we have dropped things, and being helped to feel good after we might have embarrassed ourselves, we treat those who gave us their time, with abandon when they get older?

How do we really treat our parents and grandparents as they seem to require more and more attention?

Let's remember to treat those who took care of us when we were children with respect and dignity, like they did us.

Guilty By Accusation

How many times have rumors helped you,
form your opinion of someone?
Reputations, families, and lives have been destroyed;
simply because of petty jealousies and ignorance.
If you want to hurt someone individually or in a group,
all you have to do is make an *accusation*.

Accusation without proof,
is a coward's way,
of attacking someone,
without being responsible,
for your actions.

Why do some people listen to rumors, or gossip about others?
Rather than go to the person, and just ask them any questions they might have.
What does it say about us that we will let a rumor regarding someone form our opinion about that person, when in many situations we have never even met them.
Starting, or repeating accusations, is a coward's way to hurt people. It shows how shallow minds deal with accountability and responsibility.
If we do it ourselves, how do we teach our children not to be prejudice or judgmental? Our children listen to us talk about others behind their backs and we wonder where they get it from as they get older.

There are those who want to believe the worst in people. If they think they know something no one else does, and can say it first, it makes them feel important. A big part of their lives are spent talking about others, usually about things that are not true, and the person being talked about cannot defend themselves.

The rumors and accusations can stop with us. As adults, if we ask ourselves what role do we play in demonstrating our maturity, leadership, and parenting skills will go a long way in setting an example to the younger generation to stop character assassination of those who do not deserve it.

Thanks Firemen!

I want to give a personal hardy thanks to the Decatur/Hamilton Fire Department for their fast and efficient action on Feb 5th 2008.
I know this is a little late, but as a merchant/shop owner in Decatur the need for a fire department to respond urgently and efficiently has never been so obvious.
The sacrifice the department members make on each call is greatly appreciated and their willingness to put themselves in danger for our safety cannot be expressed enough.
A simple thanks, seems so inadequate- so I say it again.

THANKS!

This week is a reminder that many times we take the services that Public Safety Officers provide for granted.

Most times the principles involved are the ones who thank the Policemen and Firemen who helped them. Although they really appreciate the acknowledgement of what they do, they get a lot of those.
A lot of times, the feeling they get from some of us, are "It's their job and it's what they get paid to do, so, why should I give them an extra thanks. No one gives me extra thanks to me, for doing my job."

My response would be, if you put your life on the line every time you came to work, an extra thank you now and then, would feel pretty good.

If we put ourselves in their position, it makes a much larger impact on them to be recognized by random citizens, families or groups, than just the individual that they help at any given time.

It would be nice if a group, like a school classroom, a community of neighbors, or just and individual would randomly send our Public Service Officers a thank you card, a batch of cookies, or a pie just to say thanks.

Perception

When you change the way
you look at things,
The things you look at
change.

How many of us judge a person,
by how they look and act,
without taking time,
to get to know them?

The Cowboy Poet Will Rogers once said,
"I never met a man I didn't like."

Does that mean he liked everyone he ran into? No, it doesn't.
It does mean, however, that he took the time to get to know the ones he did meet and, in doing so, discovered something about that person that they had in common.

If we can take the time and change the way we look at things and others, the things and others we look at would change.

If we choose the role in life of not being a judgmental person, we will then be open to the discovery of new things. When we are open to new things and experiences, it will make us better people.

As adults, we must view as many different options in life as we can, and a big one is to look at things with an open mind and be fair when forming opinions of others.

Forced to Agree

If you would just listen to me,
you would understand what I am talking about,
then you would *agree* with me.

How many of us are beat up emotionally,
by others who will not accept the fact,
that we do understand them;
we just do not *agree* with them.

It's amazing how many of the people we know think we do not understand what they are talking about. For some reason, they do not give us the credit God gave us.

Some do not accept the fact that we do have a brain and really do understand what they are talking about. We just choose not to agree with them.

How often do we hear, "Let me tell you again", or "Will you listen to me this time?", or "Let me re-phrase it and you may understand it better."

Sometimes, it may even get to the point where we have to tell them we do not want to hear anymore. Rather than *them* understanding that we do not agree, they get mad, get defensive, and start to accuse us of not listening.

We all have things we feel passionately about and want others to join in that passion and support us, but not everyone will. That doesn't mean they are not listening.

A question you may ask yourself is, "Do I want others to agree with me because I brow-beat them and it doesn't matter whether they agree or not OR do I want to know that they are listening to me and are not afraid to give me their honest opinion, even if they disagree with what I am saying?"

Hammer & Nail

If the only tool in your personal toolbox is a **hammer**,
everything you deal with,
will look like a **nail**.

How many times have we become so upset with an issue,
that we can't seem to figure it out, or get our way,
that we become angry and physical?
Solving problems with anger and violence,
will only end in trouble,
and the problem never goes away.

"If you say that about me again, I'll beat you up".

You expect that from small children. I refer to them (some adults) as children simply because the 3, 4, and 5 year olds I see act just that way. Most children learn different ways to deal with issues by the time they reach adulthood...

What is surprising is, when you hear the saying above from an adult. When that happens, we question what kind of role model they are for the younger people in their lives.

How do we expect our children to have more problem solving tools in their personal tool box if the only tool that we, as caregivers, provide is a hammer?

If our children hear shouting, cussing, shoving, and hitting between the adults in their lives, isn't it all but expected that they will grow up to have the same lack of problem solving skills?

If we want our children to have better personal and working relationships, then they will need to look at the role we play in teaching them mature problem solving in real life situations. Our children start to learn good communication and problem solving skills through the examples demonstrated by their parents.

As parents, we need to be very careful about the example we are showing our children.

Frustration

I expected more from you,
and it *frustrates* me,
when you act like that.

Whose or what expectations,
are we being asked to live up to?
The day we become 18,
are we expected to behave as an adult?

Are we held responsible for things?
Others think we should know?
But, haven't been taught yet?

It frustrates me when you do not act your age.

How many times have I told you?

"You are not a kid, anymore; you need to stop acting like one."

We, as adults, have expectations and perceptions we place on others. If they are friends, relatives, or our children we expect certain behaviors out of them.

At a point, we presume that people at certain ages should know certain things. I don't know many 17 year olds who really know that the day they turn 18, ALL the rules change. Why is it we get so frustrated with them when, in most cases, we have never told them about the change? In most cases, we tell them, "things are going to change when you turn 18", without any more explanation. Even our attitude changes toward our own children when they turn 18. This can be very confusing to the new young adult. Why do we get frustrated with those who do not know the rules?

No matter what our age, we will make mistakes, if we have to figure things out or don't know things and no one teaches, mentors, or trains us. We also can become very frustrated being held accountable for things we were not explained or trained about.

As parents, supervisors, managers, or in any leadership position, we must learn tolerance and patience.

When we have expectations of our children, employees or managers there must be teaching and training to match those expectations.

Listen to the Wind

"When was the last time you stopped and
listened to the wind?
Listening to the wind demands
you give yourself permission
to take 10 minutes out of your life
and just listen to the sounds
around you. You may actually
hear something new and exciting."

Bill Orr,
A friend of mine

The wind brings all the sounds of our life to us, if we just listen. In a house full of children, have you ever just stopped what you were doing and just listened to the sounds? For anyone who has ever sat under a tree in the woods and just listened to the wind blowing through the tree tops, it gave us so much solitude.

If you stop thinking about all you should, or need to, be doing and just listen, you will hear kids playing, food cooking, the TV or radio, cars going by, the heater or air conditioner running, and if you sit long enough you will be able to tune them out and
just hear peace.

If you practice this long enough, you will be able pick what you want to hear. It would be great just to be able to hear the sounds of your own breathing and heart beat.

For any of this to happen, you must give yourself permission to take some personal, private time and stop worrying for a few minutes each day. By doing this, you may discover something new and exciting about yourself, those around you, or your environment.

As we grow older, our world is so full of activity and noise, most of us can't remember a real quiet time and, if we do, it was a long time ago. When we remember those times, it was either up a tree, by ourselves, just resting and thinking, or sitting on a dock looking into the water, or something similar, if not just enjoying the privacy of our rooms. What made us stop doing those small things that made us so happy, even for only a few minutes at a time? In this day and age, there is something new and exciting about quiet.

Good People to do Nothing

"All it takes for violence and
Substance abuse to grow is for the
Good people to do nothing."

Edmund Burke

Why is it we think by not holding a wrongdoer or
someone hurting themselves or others accountable that it
is the right thing to do?

When do we say, "I/We have had enough?"

Why is it that when something inappropriate or illegal happens, most people say nothing? That does not stop us from saying "they shouldn't be doing that", or "why doesn't someone stop that?", or "where are the police?" or any number of similar comments.
The police are not called because good people do nothing.

Why is it we think by not holding a wrongdoer, or someone hurting themselves, accountable is the right thing to do?
When do we say, "I/We have had enough?"

We tend to only become involved, when whatever happens, happens directly to us or our family.
For some reason we have this "them vs. us" mentality, when it comes to the authority.
It's like we are still kids saying and thinking,
"I'm not going to tell on them. Let them find out the hard way."
Why is finding out the hard way suppose to fix things?
I think that saying, and that idea, is for people who don't want to take responsibility for our brothers and sisters.
With most adults being afraid, or just not willing to get involved, we wonder where our children learn it.

It is not okay to be a convenient good person.
If we are going to talk the talk we also need to walk the walk

Be a Good Winner, Be a Good Loser

You should strive to be good at both winning and losing,
or you will not really be good at either one of them.

A good loser has personal integrity and ethics,
For without them, he will also be a poor winner.

Everyone would like to be a winner, and most of us work on being a winner most of the time. Winning makes us feel good, and puts us at the center of attention. These things improve our self-esteem and self-confidence. Being a winner also encourages us to try more challenging goals throughout our life.

That is fine, but how do you handle losing on occasion? A lot of people take losing as failure and by seeing themselves as a failure, can become depressed, and start to lose their self-esteem and self-confidence.

With a positive attitude, losing is a way to teach us how to lose with dignity. Losing teaches us that what we were doing did not work, but if we continue to be motivated and keep working on whatever it was that caused us to fail, we will become successful.

By becoming a good loser, with a positive attitude, it will also make you a good winner.

ARE YOU BLIND?

Are you blind with your eyes open?
Do you take time, or find a way,
to look at the big picture
and hear the whole story?

Do you only see, or hear, what you want to?
Are you a person with honesty and integrity?
A person who continues a rumor is the
same as the person who started it.

So,

What role do you play?

"Therefore, I speak to them in parables, because seeing they do not see, and hearing they do not hear, nor do they understand."

Matthew 13:13

Author unknown

Seeing things that are going on around you is not the problem. What can become a problem is seeing something that may require attention and not doing anything about it. If no one knows we saw it, we can deny seeing it and do nothing about it.

Are you a person with selective hearing? Do you hear what you what to hear? It is so easy to say, "Oh, I didn't hear you." Most of the time you, and the person talking, know you heard what was said, but chose not to hear it.

Why is it that we see and hear what we want to when it suits us; for example, if something serious or injurious happens? What keeps us from telling someone or reporting it to the authorities?
Yet, when something is said that may or may not be true about someone, we feel the need to pass it on, regardless of whether or not it's true.

How is it we are fine about spreading lies and rumors, but when it comes to reporting something wrong to someone in authority, and helping someone, we won't do it?
When we see and hear someone spreading lies and rumors, why is it we don't tell them to stop? Our mind tells us what to do, but our heart tells us if it is right or wrong. Why do we not listen?
What role do you play in being a person of honesty and integrity?

Be Better Than Yesterday

You should not work on being better than anyone else.
You should work on being ***better than you were yesterday***.

Don't just settle for being
OK at life.
Every day should be a learning, and growing experience,
and ***you*** should be a positive teacher and role model.

If you always work on being better than the people next door,
or the kid in the desk next to you.
When do you have time to be yourself?
If you will work on yourself,
and work on doing, or learning, something new each day,
you will make yourself a little better each day.
By doing this, you continually improve, day by day.

Even if you fail occasionally, at least you will have learned a way, whatever
you were doing, how not to do it.
Learning, how not to do something,
is what stops you from making the same mistake twice.

It is OK to compete against other people.
Where it becomes a problem,
is when you try to become better than others.
For example, an Olympic champion runner is called
the fastest runner in the world, not the best runner.

The only person important enough,
for you to continually work on being better than,
is yourself.

Never Be Ashamed

A person should **never be ashamed**,
to say he has been wrong.
Which is also saying,
that he is **wiser** today,
than he was yesterday.

Losing is really winning,
when you build character and maturity,
from the experience.

Why are we unable to admit we are wrong?
When being wrong teaches us so much?

If we are taught, at an early age, to look at the role we play,
in the things we do, then, when losing,
we would look at what role we played and how we played it.
By looking at our role,
we would see what caused us to not be successful,
and to look at how we might do things differently.

If we are unable to lose,
we can become afraid to try anything new.
Once we get into that pattern of behavior,
we no longer have adventure in our lives.

Those who are not afraid to try new things,
and *maybe* fail, will continue to grow and learn.
Life with them will continue to be challenging and exciting.

Losing, gives us dignity and keeps us humble.
It gives us motivation, to study the ones who do win,
and allows us to learn from others.
We learn, not only from their mistakes,
but from their successes as well.
Losing would be a great opportunity to learn,
if only we were taught,
how to accept losing with a positive attitude.

Listening

The skill of *listening*, and not judging,
seems to be a dying skill.
Many are confused, about the differences,
in getting information,
having an opinion,
and making a judgment.

An opinion is made,
by those who ask questions, listen,
and see for themselves with an open mind.
A judgment is made,
by those who never ask, or see,
but only hear what they want to hear,
because it suits their already preconceived opinion.

Our skill, in listening, is learned when we are very young.
If our parents listen to us, and ask us questions,
this teaches us to ask questions, and listen,
before forming our own opinions.

Many people today are very quick to make a judgment,
about something or someone, by talking to that person,
instead of asking questions and listening to what is said.

Those who do not have good listening skills, many times,
find themselves in situations, where they act, or make a decision, without
all the information.
This can make their jobs very hard, when others stop talking to them,
because they have shown they don't listen anyway.
They have a habit of saying, "No one told me how to do it,
or no one explained it to me." Had they listened,
they would have been told the same as everyone else.
They just did not listen.

Some also stop listening, when what is being said,
does not match, or may contradict,
what someone, they trust, has told them in the past.

Having good listening and communication skills
will make our personal life, and working environment,
so much more, pleasant and easier.

Secrets and Friends

We are told something in confidence,
and asked to keep it **secret**.
The news is very exciting, or juicy,
so we feel we can tell our very best *friend*.

What most of us do not think about,
is our very best *friend*, also has a very best *friend*,
And it may not be us.
They feel, they can tell their very best *friend*,
for the same reasons you told them.

This is how a lot of gossip and rumors start.

We should learn about having and telling secrets when we are young, but we don't.

As children, it can make us feel important when we think we know something no one else knows. Just knowing a secret is powerful.

It seems, as we get older, we forget that secrets never stay secrets very long. We see or hear something we shouldn't and we just can't seem to keep it to ourselves. We tell a friend, our girlfriend, or a fellow employee, and we do it in confidence. Our friend tells his friend, our girlfriend tells her girlfriend, and our fellow employee tells other employees

When we start telling secrets, about things we don't know are true, it's not a secret; it is now a rumor.
Before you tell your friend what you think may be a secret,
make sure you have all the information,
so that it doesn't matter if it gets repeated.

You also do not want to get the reputation,
of someone who cannot keep information confidential,
whether it is told to you by a friend, or an employer.
Once you establish that you can be told personal or sensitive information,
by a friend or employer,
you then become someone others will trust.

Freedom and Independence

As much as some complain,
and as bad as some seem to think it is,
I am very **proud**
to wake up each morning,
in **America**.

God Bless,
all our service men & women,
past, present, and future.
Please, don't ever stop doing your job.
Help protect our *Freedom and Independence*.

This is one thing, I am *very passionate* about.

I believe, it is a shame, for anyone, to protest
the men and women in the military.
If you do not like the military, that is your choice,
You have a couple of choices to make.

1. Don't join the military service.
2. Join an organization that legally combats our military.
3. If you do not want to do one of those,

Then just **shut up**,
And let others make their own choices.

It's like people who do not get involved, and do not vote, then
Bitch about what the government does, or does not do.

I believe, there are parents who have lost sons and daughters, while in the
military, and become anti – military because of that loss.
By becoming anti – military, they are dishonoring the decision their son's
and daughter's, as adults, have made. The real sad thing is, if their son or
daughter had come home a hero, they would have been proud of them for
volunteering and doing their duty.

America has always aided the oppressed and down trodden
and, I hope, will never stop doing that.
Our military personnel understand this, and support it.

God Bless all the men and women, who give, of themselves,
To defend this county and its allies.

Two Ears

We are all born with *two* ears and *one* mouth.
We should be listening **twice**
as much as we **talk**!

This one is very simple, in theory, but almost impossible in practice.

How many of us have talked ourselves into all kinds of trouble, some of it very serious, and if we would have just kept our mouth shut, and listened, everything would have been fine?

How many times, when someone is trying to explain something, or give us directions, do we interrupt, while they are still talking, by telling that person we understand them.
Again, we should have been *listening,* instead of talking.

Listening has become something our youth, have a hard time learning and practicing. I think many believe, if they can talk loud, and long enough, they can beat others down. A lot of that behavior is because they do not want to hear the truth or anything that may contradict what they want to do, so they do not want to listen.

If you really listen, without so much talking, you might have heard, that you were able to do what you wanted, but you continued talking and interrupting. This upset the ones trying to work with you, so everyone ended up getting upset, and you don't get what you wanted, all because you did more talking than listening.

Dogs-vs.-People

Dogs love their friends, and will bite their enemies.
Quite unlike *people*, who like *dogs*, will bite their enemies.
But unlike *dogs*, in most cases,
People end up biting their friends as well.

How do we end up turning our friends into our enemies?
Are we able to honor and respect friendship?

There are very few people who have a friend who will really stick with them through thick and thin.

We select our friends mostly because they have the same likes and dislikes we have. When those likes and dislikes get challenged we can focus on what is challenging us and forget about our friendship. Are we saying, "You can be my friend as long as you agree with me."?

It seems so many of us haven't learned to accept those who will become friends of ours, but still may have a different opinion than ours.

If we all agreed on the same things; what a boring world it would be. The only person who we never have a disagreement with is ourselves, and it isn't any fun being alone all the time.

We should remember real friends aren't very available and are hard to find. Friends should be honored and respected even if they have a different view or opinion than ours.

Choices:
Follower or Leader

When we are in our early teens, and start to grow up,
We make *choices*; whether we are going to be a *follower* or a *leader*.

If we are going to be *followers* (and it is OK; the world needs them)
Then we must *choose* whom we are going to follow.
Does the person, we *choose* to follow, have the same goals, morals and ethics we have, or we wish to have?
As a *follower*, does the person, we *choose* to follow, have the best interest of those following in mind, or does the *leader* have their own agenda, one that does not include those who are following them?

Does the person, we *choose* to follow, know right from wrong?
Does the person even care about such things?
As a *follower*, am I going to be held responsible for someone else's decisions and, if I am, is it going to be something that I am proud to be connected with, or something that embarrasses me, or shames me.
If we *choose* to be a *follower*, those are important things we need to think about.

If your *choice* is to be a *leader*,
What kind of *leader* do you want to be?
Do you want to be one, others like to follow?
Or one, others have to follow?

Do you want the responsibility of having others follow you,
because you have the same goals and they see you as a positive role model?

Do you understand, and respect, community values and
encourage your followers to believe the same.
Do you believe rules are to be broken if you don't like them?
Do you respect, or disrespect, authority, i.e. parents, teachers, police or other adults, and do you teach those who follow you to do the same?

Do you agree with those in authority to their face, then cuss and laugh about them behind their backs, and teach those who follow and trust you to do the same? Will you then accept the consequences for them, if they get into trouble for what you taught them?

Whether you are a Leader or Follower, there will consequences for your decisions and actions, and those consequences can be positive or negative, depending on your *choices*.
Leaders and Followers need to know that not all consequences are negative, a lot of consequences are positive.
(A nice paycheck after a week's work is a positive consequence.)

As a Leader or Follower, you need to think for yourself,
because if you *choose* to follow the wrong leader,
or you are a negative leader, your *choices* will directly affect
those around you and, in most cases, the ones you love, who may end up being really hurt and/or paying for something they had nothing to do with.

Patient or Enabling?

If, as a parent I show *patience* to another person (partner, friend, or child) who is inappropriate or pushing the boundaries, hoping they will change their behavior, am I being ***Patient*** or am I ***Enabling***?

I know having *patience* is a good thing, and I like it when others are ***patient*** with me.

Do the others (partner, friends, or child) understand I am being ***patient***, or do they think I am ignoring (***enabling***) their behavior and they are getting away with something?

Do we understand when our *patience* turns to being an *enabler*?

When do we say, I have been ***patient*** long enough?
What you are doing has to stop?
If we can't do that, we then become an *enabler*.

Most parents, employers, or supervisors want only the best, for those that are still growing and willing to learn.

We are patient with young children, new employees, or anyone exposed to a new environment.

With our children, we are patient with them because they have so much to learn, but after we have explained the same thing, more than once, and they seem to be ignoring us, and we do nothing?

It is then that we become an enabler.

The same with new employees, we are patient with them, while they are learning a new job or skill, but after awhile, if they don't seem to be learning, and we don't do something, then we become enabling.

The skill is figuring out when we move,
from *being patient to an enabler.*

It is easier, as an employer, you will have a written policy of training, and job performance. If the employee does not follow the policy, he is given warnings, and if they do not motivate the employee, he is let go.

When working with our children, we parents seem to have a hard time figuring that out. If we had been consistent in our approach, from an early age, we may not become an enabler as they grow older. Most of the time, we wait way too long, and by the time we decide to do something about it, our children have been enabled for so long, that they resist any kind of behavioral change.

One key, to find the balancing point, is to be consistent in our parenting, and to set boundaries as to allowable behavior.

Life could, would, and should, be so much easier.

Is it working?

If what you are doing, or the situation you are in, **_is not working_**,
You may need to look at changing what you are doing.

"If you keep doing what you've always done,
You'll always get what you've always gotten."

John C. Maxwell

Why is it most men, and some women, are so stubborn, that we will keep working, on whatever we are working on, till it drives us nuts, or end up throwing it away?

It would be a different if, by continuing to work on what we were doing, we were making even a little progress every now and then.

Insanity definition: "Doing the same thing over and over and over and expecting different results."

Sometimes, we should put what we are doing away for a little while and come back to it later. Or, ask someone else to look at and see if there is another way.

There is a lot to be said for talking to others about something giving us trouble.

If what you are doing in a relationship, either personal or working, is not working, then you must honestly look at the role you are playing in it.

If you want to keep that relationship, you are the one who must change, and if you have made every attempt to change, and you are still unable to change, then you need to leave that relationship and find another, that suits you.

Life is, and technology is, constantly changing and we need to be able to change with it, or it will seem like we are continually beating our heads against a wall.

Sometimes, we only need to make small changes, but it keeps us up with what is going on around us.

Encourage Creativity

Resist telling people how something should be done.

Instead, tell them what needs to be done.
They will often surprise you with *creative solutions*.

There is a difference between telling and encouraging people to do things.

Even children do not like to be told what to do, all the time, instead show them, and encourage them, to learn, and then acknowledge them when they become successful.

Most adults I know, when given a job, and then told what needs to be done, like to be left alone to accomplish it. Most will also ask for help, if they get into a situation that is difficult, or new.

J.P. Getty was quoted, "Find the guy who is doing his job and sitting down more than the rest. See what he is doing and copy it for the rest." This would not only make work smoother for the rest, but would allow the company to increase production.

A lot of people, children and adults, are more interested in doing a good job, and if allowed, can become very creative and ingenious with new, and possibly faster, ways, of getting their work done.

A good parent, or manager, should allow certain latitudes when assigning tasks and jobs. By giving a little latitude and supporting them to be successful, it will create a lot of pride and satisfaction.

How to become a Bully?

(or in other words a coward)

1. Pick on others smaller or weaker than you, who cannot defend themselves.
2. Pick on others not as smart as you, and who cannot verbally defend themselves
3. Pick on others who have a physical disability, and cannot defend themselves.
4. Pick on others with an intellectual disability, and cannot defend themselves.
5. Pick on others who are a different race or religion, and due to their beliefs will not fight back.
6. Pick on those smarter than you, but who are smaller, and cannot defend themselves.

When you become good at these things, and a few more, you can be proud to call yourself a qualified **Bully**. You will be known by your peers, and adults, as someone who will not pick on anyone your own size, only younger and smaller people. You will also be known as someone who will not pick on anyone who might hit back.

People are not born bullies, but learn how, at an early age.

You can't explain, to a young child, how to be a bully, they learn from seeing. The older male in the house, bullies the women, and smaller people, and the older male keeps doing it, so why would they not do it as well?

A lot of domestic violence perpetrators learn from watching dad hit, and beat up, mom, when they were young children.
Abusive behavior can be seen in young children who push around younger children, hit younger children, and beat up on smaller children. This behavior continues as they grow into adulthood.

When the young boys become men, they stay the same, while the world changes. They change from bullies to batterers.

> "The only time a batterer feels like a man is
> when he is beating a woman."

Tina Geotz, Domestic Violence Coach

As parents, we need to be sensitive, to the example we are showing our children, on how to treat women, and younger people, and how we allow ourselves to be treated. If we set an example, on how we allow ourselves to be abused, our children see that as well.
Our daughters can grow up thinking, that's how women
should be treated.

We should not forget, behaviors are learned,
and parents are the first teachers our children have.

Environmental Awareness vs. Environmental Conditioning©

You are sitting on your front porch and you watch a cougar go by, slowly, as if it were on the prowl, you watch it go into the distance, stop, then it slowly turns around and faces your direction.

Inch by inch it starts towards you, picking up speed with every foot, until it draws in front of you, that's when two of the three occupants open fire.

Lucky for you, you are aware of your environment, having grown up with an acute sense (like a fine tuned sixth sense) of self-preservation.

Your gut feeling was that something was not right. So by the time, the car was just about in front of you, you were already off the porch, and on your way around the side of the house. So once again, environmental conditioning had saved your life.

This story came about because a friend (who is very much an environmentalist), and I were talking, about being environmentally aware.

How good it is for the kids of today, be exposed to it, and learn about protecting the environment. It can survive, which will in turn, allow them (the kids) to survive better, for generations to come.

She was an environmentalist and I was a juvenile counselor.

We ended up in a unique conversation.

We both understood overcrowding and poverty, in our larger cities, is an environment needing to be addressed, but we looked at it from different views. She looked at it from the point of view of trees, grass, and nature.

All things we are losing on a daily basis, and if we don't get our youth involved, there may come a time, when the environment may not recover.

1On this point, I completely agreed with her, but I said, the youth I work With, are more worried about surviving in their community, at this time, and are very environmentally aware, or as I called it environmentally conditioned.

I worked very hard to explain how I was thinking. As far as a long-term big picture for our earth and the future, I do agree with my friend, that all of us need to be Environmentally Aware.

I tried to explain, if you are a youth, worried about surviving today, and what may happen to you or your family tomorrow.

You are not thinking about the earth's environment, now or tomorrow.

You know the environment you live, and in that environment, you know what it will take for survival. There are groups that hang together for protection, or for what they think is being accepted, because it's their way of surviving in their environment.

It's just like you heard about in one of your school classes.

They were talking about the young animals in the wild, and how they are taught. You learn to stay close together, with other like young.

This is so, as they grow up, they all learn the same kind of survival techniques for their environment, and by doing that, they may grow up to be adults, take a mate and reproduce, which is really the only focus they have. They know they can only protect each other from being killed, or seriously hurt, by staying in groups. By presenting this image, they may secure their future.

They also understand that by walking around alone, they are subject to be harmed or killed. By learning to stay in groups, of at least two, and not to stray too far from the group, they may be safe and live another day.

As a student you may have been thinking how much it sounded like your neighborhood. The difference is (unlike humans), with the animals, this environment will never change. We as humans have the ability to change our environment
or move to one that is not as violent. It was explained that, in the wild, it is pure animal instinct. The PARENTS teach survival of the fittest, as soon as the young are born. The biggest, prettiest male gets the most food and the most females, until another male comes along and pushes him out, by chasing him off or killing him.

After listening to the speaker the young boy thought, they are talking about my community. He had no real understanding about the environmental awareness that they were referring to. He did have enough understanding that the feeling of the animals and his were just about the same.
The things he, and his sisters, were taught by their mom and dad were very similar. You must protect the young, and it is the women's role to do that.
Young men protected themselves in groups, but at the same time, you have to be the biggest and best (have the most to offer) to attract partners.
You are starting to understand, that there are two different environments, and both are real. The one you live in, has buildings that can be very bad, and at times are almost more dangerous than the streets.

The streets themselves are cement, with abandoned cars, and vacant lots, with garbage all around, a lot of the time. This is your environment, it is very real and all you are trying to do, is survive. Being the biggest and prettiest males allows you the best chance of survival, and generally, gives you the most females, so you can have the most children, because at some point, you learned that producing kids is a sign of manhood.

You don't quite know what the attack, while you were sitting on the porch, was all about, but sometimes it's, as simple as, a young cub growing up and showing off for the rest pack. He is showing he can take care of himself and has earned the right to be part of the community.
Although the attempted killing, of the cub and the young man, are similar, in that they are both learning how to survive. It has been inbred in one and learned by the other, one is able to stop and the other one isn't.

You are starting to wonder just how far we have really come. You hear stuff, on radio and TV, about protecting the environment, by doing this and that, so generations to come will have an opportunity to survive. All the time you thought, you were doing, just what you were taught.
I am, you thought, protecting my group, my family, and the area I live, from other groups, who may kill us and take our things. I am just doing my part, to be Environmental Aware.

A young person can grow up in an environment of "What Role Did I Play" and with understanding that I can make a choice, at one time or another, and be held accountable for that choice. That the actions and behaviors I exhibit are learned, and not inbred, as in the animal world, but as a human I do have choices.

As parents you need to ask yourself, "What Role Did We Play", in supporting our children, to understand "What Role They Play" in their lives and the future.

Who or What?

Do we decide what is right or wrong?
Because of **Who** (maybe one of our friends) says so?
Or, are we able to make up our own minds?
Sometimes we are so caught up in,
Who's right and **Who's** wrong,
That we forget,
What's right and **What's** wrong.
Wrong is wrong, and it doesn't matter.
Who says it?

Sometimes, we make people so important that we don't think they would do anything wrong.
When these same people do something wrong, we think, they wouldn't do that, but if they say it is OK, then it should be.

We know, in our heart, what is right or wrong, but sometimes we are so influenced, by someone, that the black and white, of right and wrong, becomes gray.

Sometimes, when the competition gets so strong, that we have to prove another person wrong, we do things that are questionable, and we may even cheat. We didn't hurt anyone, but what we did was wrong, and we knew it.

This should be the beginning, of questioning our ethics.

Being ethical means, it doesn't matter who says nor does anything, you know what is right or wrong, and you will do what is right.

Ethics is doing the right thing when no one is watching.

Happiness

Understand, that **happiness** is not based,
on possessions, power, or prestige,
but on relationships,
with people you love and respect.

Possessions get old and fall apart.
Power comes and goes: it never lasts.
Prestige is dependent upon others opinion.

True happiness costs nothing,
does not get old,
will last forever,
and does not require the opinion of others.

The old saying, "Money cannot buy happiness," was true then, and is still true today.

Possessions can bring you instant gratification, and will make you happy for a little while. The happiness with possessions, may not last till you get your new possession home. You may enjoy it for while, until it starts to cost you more to keep it working, replace parts, or replace it with a newer model.

Power comes, with a lot of responsibility. Others will generally want things from you, plus you will never know who your friends are. Many will say, you are their friend because of what it can get them; it makes others feel good, to be a friend of power. Lose that power and see how many hang around.

Prestige is, generally, short lived, and can make you the center of attention, only while you are able to maintain the quality, rank and influence needed. Once any of those is gone, so are your "friends" and "supporters".

True happiness cost nothing, does not get old, will last forever, and does not require the opinion of others.

FREEDOM

Whether we like it or not, someone is always,
going to challenge our way of life.

If you are not prepared, to do anything, to support the future
FREEDOM, for you or your family, do not make fun of, or complain
about, those who do. Men and women, you do not know, will put
themselves in harm's way, so you can complain, and cry, about things
you do not like.

**May God Bless our past, present and future Americans
who choose to defend us all.**

As a veteran, this one is a very easy topic to write about.

We in this country have more individual freedoms, rights and privacy, than then any other country in the world.
These God-given privileges were not handed to us; we had to work and fight for them, from the beginning of our nation.

There are so many now, who have had these hard fought freedoms all of their life, and they take them for granted. Having freedoms is all they know, and they have never had to do anything to earn, or keep, the freedoms, they so easily use, and abuse.

I wish every man and woman, of legal age, had to serve at least 2 years in the military. That way, they may learn about the freedoms we enjoy, and what it really took for them, to have these
God-given privileges.

We have so many influential pseudo-intellectuals, who will sacrifice any, or all, pride, or self-esteem, to go so far as to give up some of those freedoms, by believing talking (surrendering) to the enemy, and being nice, that they will continue to live as usual, like the world does not change. Those people have no idea, we do not ask, or beg, to have our freedoms. Our ancestors have done the fighting for us. All we have to do is maintain, and defend. What makes our country, (with all its' faults) what it is today.

God Bless America

Life vs. Death

If **death** has no meaning, then **life** has no meaning.

If we have just bought a ticket, to our favorite band or activity,
and a relative, or friend, of ours dies.

Do we tell ourselves, "They're dead anyway,
So it won't matter to them, if I go."?

If we do not acknowledge them after **death**,
Then we give no meaning to their **life**.

How do we feel about attending a funeral?

Do we attend because we knew that person in life, and wanted to recognize, and celebrate, that life, by being respectful in their death?

Do we attend funerals because we feel obligated, by relatives and friends, but feel without that pressure we probably wouldn't have attended?

Have we thought about that person's life? What kind of person they were? Do we focus on the times they upset us, or are we mature enough to look at the big picture? Do we take time to learn about them?

Do we take the time to recognize the accomplishments they achieved during their lives, and acknowledge them after death?

By acknowledging them after death,
We give meaning to their life.

Note to Good Samaritans:

For security reasons,
Walter Reed Hospital will not be accepting cards, for wounded or
disabled veterans this year, without a specific name.
To send cards to a Wounded or Disabled Veteran,
for the holiday season, please send them to:

Holiday Mail For Heroes
P.O. Box 5456
Capitol Heights,
MD. 20791-5456

All cards must be postmarked, no later than Dec. 10.
Cards **should not** be mailed to,
Walter Reed Army Medical Center.

This note was made, to let readers know, that during the holiday season, and due to the new security system, there are strict guide lines, for sending mail to veterans.

If you have a veteran in the VA system, you should see what restrictions there are to send mail, packages, and gifts.

Do not get upset, if it is a little frustrating in the beginning, as there are some real sub-intellectual, un-patriotic midgets out there.

The only way they have learned to express themselves, is to make the lives, of those they disagree with, difficult and fearful.

The government has had to establish, and enforce, rules, to protect the same people who fought, got wounded, and died, so their descendents can talk and act with freedom.

Being a Victim

We are *victims,* for a lot of reasons.
As children, we are the *victim*,
of a lot of different things out of our control,
and many times it affects us,
and how we view others, as we grow up.

"The role we play changes with time and circumstances,
While, we don't always have control,
over the role we are placed in,
We do have control, over the way we play it."

Mike Siver, Performance Coach

How much more of a *victim* can one be?
If you're whole life was spent,
Working for good and spreading love?
You were still arrested, crucified and buried in a tomb,
With no marker on whom you were.

If that person doesn't consider himself a *victim*,
Then, as an adult, I have nothing in the world to feel victimized
about, unless I want to stay a *victim* and
Feel sorry for myself and get sympathy.

It is the nature of human beings, to help others who are less fortunate then themselves, and most people will even help more than once.

This can become a problem when it is abused.
There are those, who are just plain beggars, and choose not to work. They live, on sob stories, and work very hard to get the generous people, to feel sorry for them.

We all have hard times in our lives, but for some they think their problems should be everybody else's, and they expect you, to at least pay them more attention, or give them a break.
They are so into being a victim, which they believe if you aren't complaining about a problem, that you really don't have a problem; if you did, you would be complaining also.

We all have people we love die, have accidents, get sick, or any number of things. It is how we deal with them,
That shows our maturity.

We choose what role we play in our lives,
and it changes at a moment's notice.
Some of the changes are good and some not so good,
but it's how we deal with them that shows our maturity level.
We can accept whatever happened and move on, or, we tell everyone our troubles, and choose the role of a victim, to feel sorry for ourselves, and expect everyone else to as well.

Be positive in your life.
Pick a positive role to play,
After all, it is your choice.

Learn

"Listen, and *learn* from the mistakes of others...
You won't live long enough to make all of them yourself."

Dan Morrissette,
Retired Toymaker

The old saying was, and still is…
"You should learn from your mistakes."

We make mistakes, as children, because we sometimes don't understand what some adults tell us. Then, we make mistakes as teens, and young adults, because we think we are better than that.

It's not until we reach a certain age (different for everyone), that we start to understand another old saying…
"My parents get smarter the older I get".

It's at this point, we start to listen to adults, when they tell us, "you shouldn't do that, it would be a mistake…
Or it might be better if you try it this way instead."
Or any number of things they have learned
from their own, and others, mistakes.

As Mr. Morrissette so amiable says, "Listen and learn."

D.U.I.

I don't understand the ad on TV that say's
"Friends don't let Friends Plead Guilty".

Is that saying, friends *should* let friends drive drunk,
just don't plead guilty if you get caught?

What kind of message is that sending?
If you can afford a Lawyer, plead not guilty,
and buy your way out of being
responsible for your actions.

I thought, friends don't let friends drive drunk,
and if they did anyway, friends tell those friends,
to be accountable for their actions ,
and admit what they did wrong,
then deal with it like the adult,
they are trying to be.

I wrote this one after watching the ad on television saying:
"Friends don't let Friends Plead Guilty".

I felt, and still feel, it was a marketing ploy, by a legal firm, to solicit clients, from those who choose to drink and drive.

The reason I oppose this ad is, I thought it was sending a completely wrong, and dangerous, message.

For a legal firm, or anyone for that matter, to imply that it's ok to not take responsibility, for ones actions, is against all the principles that the majority of us have.

I think I made my feelings very clear, when I placed my comments, on the previous page, in the local newspaper.
It may have been a coincidence, but shortly after I printed my feelings, the ad was pulled from the television networks.

Advice vs. Lecture

Most of the time, the differences between *Advice* and a *Lecture*,
is the perception of the receiver of the information.
The information may be the very best thing for them,
but they will never know, because they do not want to hear it,
and will take it as a lecture.

That very same information may really help, and support them.
If the person would listen, with an open mind, rather than put the
information in a category of advice or lecture, take it at face value,
process it, and then make an educated decision, as to whether the
information is something they can, or cannot use.

By listening to the information with a closed mind, you are giving less
value to the person trying to help you, and giving less value to yourself,
by rejecting the person, and not the information.

When we were children, we were told what to do, by the adults around us. We somehow understood, as time went by, the adults were only trying to help us, with the advice they were trying to give us.

A couple things happen as we get older. We start to resent being given advice, and will do what we are told not to do, just to prove adults wrong. When we are given advice again, we switch off, and at some point, tell the adults not to lecture us anymore.

We have taken what is advice. Perceive it as a lecture. Then tell those trying to help to, "Stop lecturing me and leave me alone."

What we do not understand is that, we are pushing away those who are trying to help us. We then wonder when we do go ask for help, why those same people don't want to help us. We are even told, "Now that you want help, you ask, but when we wanted to help, you told us to stop. You can't take help only when you want it."
Why is it, at the time in our lives, when we need the most advice, we also reject it the most?

When we get much older, we then start to ask for help, when we need it, and we also listen to those who offer advice.
As adults, we should look at alternative ways to protect, and advise, our young teens, and adults, so as not to make them defensive, each time we talk.

Many times, it's not the message we don't hear, but the messenger we do not listen to.

Being Liked

I need to be **liked**, by my friends but, after some of the things I say, and do; I end up, not liking myself very much.

My head tells me, when we do, and say things, we are having fun, like talking, or gossiping about someone we don't like, but my heart tells me this is wrong.

When I look at myself, in my mind, I see, I am only happy on the outside, and use it to cover the sadness on the inside When I'm alone, I ask myself, "Do I put being **liked**, over the feelings of others?" and "How would I feel if it were done to me?"

If I am honest with myself, when I look in the mirror, I know the only one who needs to be happy, is me. I know I have to do the things that make me happy, so I can pass happiness on to others.

Sometimes, we look at a group of kids, or others, and wish, they would invite us, to be a part of their group.
We may find out, what they talk about, or like to do, and then do the same things, even if we don't like to do them.
Some of those things may be against our beliefs and ethics.

We all want to be accepted by our peers, and can become very unhappy if we are not. Wanting acceptance covers all age groups, so no one is exempt, from this feeling.

What matters the most, is what we think of ourselves, when the day is over. We must somehow figure out, if we want to be who we are, or do we needs acceptance so bad that we become a "wanna-be".
A "wanna-be" is someone who wants to be, or be like, someone they are not.

How far will we go, to be accepted by others?
Are you doing it for them, or yourself?

The very first person we need to make happy is ourselves, for if we are not happy inside, then no matter what we do on the outside, it will all just be one big cover-up... We can laugh on the outside and be crying on the inside.

We need to take pride in ourselves and who we are then we will have all the friends we want or need and we will not have to be anything but ourselves.
Take pride and maintain your self-esteem; in yourself, your family and your loved ones.

Making Friends

You can make more *friends* in two months,
By becoming interested,
In other people,
Than you can in two years,
By trying to get other people,
Interested in you.

How often do we want to make an impression on someone, so they will notice us? We work very hard, and spend a lot of time, getting others to become interested in us.

We believe, if we are smart, or if we are good at sports, that we will be popular, and liked by everyone.

If we only took interest in other people, took the time to get to know them, listen to what they have to say they, in turn, they would become interested in us.

The same applies to us. We are interested in those who take the time to get to know us, and listen to us with respect when we talk.

All the smarts, and physical abilities, only show what we can do, they do not show others who we are.

We find out who others are, only by getting to know them, and then becoming friends.

What do you see?

"We can complain because rose bushes have thorns,
Or rejoice because thorn bushes have roses."

Abraham Lincoln

Do we look at the worst in a situation?
Or, do we look for the best in people and situations?

Open challenge:

Please take the next 10 min to write,
5 negative things about you.

Next:

Take the next 10 min to write,
5 positive things about you.

Be honest-
which one was the easiest to do.

What do we see, when we see someone in clothes with frayed cuffs and collars? We need to understand, first impressions form our perception, of what we see.
Our perception is our reality, until it is proven differently.

Looking at a person with frayed cuffs and collars, give us the perception, that the person is probably poor, or they don't have many clothes, and wear the ones they have, a lot.

Do we keep that perception?
Do we take the time to get to know them?

For example, a person lying on a park bench sleeping covered over with an old blanket. Our perception is of a bum, with no means of income, and no place to go. The person could be a bum, or they could be an actor playing a role of a bum, and probably has more money than we do. If you had taken the time to get to know that person, you may have had a different view of what you saw.

We all have first impressions, and that helps form our opinion, of a situation or person. It is the person with maturity, who chooses not to make a final judgment, until we have a second look, or get more information to make an educated opinion.

Take the challenge to the left, and remember to think positive.

How far you go

"*How far you go* in life, depends on you being,
Tender with the young,
Compassionate with the aged,
Sympathetic with the striving,
Tolerant of the weak and strong,
Because someday in your life,
You will have been all of these."

George Washington Carver

It's a shame we have to wait, until we get older, to understand what it's like to give, and receive, empathy and sympathy.

Never forgetting, where we came from, and what it was like, when we were young, when we were sad; Remembering when we were weak, and needed support, when we were strong, and others put up with our ego, how others put up with us when we became ambitious, and became unmanageable.

Understanding that we will become aged one day, and knowing how we would like to be treated.

As Mr. Carver, so eloquently put, we all have been, or will be, in a position to receive empathy, and/or sympathy, so when we have an opportunity to render compassion, we should do so.

No Man

"I will let **no man**; drag me down so low, as to hate him."

Booker T. Washington

We have a choice, on how much;
We let others control our emotions, feelings, and actions.

Hate takes a lot of energy to maintain, and will make us tired at the end of the day.

Many of us do not understand that by maintaining a dislike, or hatred. We are letting someone else control us.

As soon as, we start to respond to another's negativity, we start to give that other person our power.
If they know, how we are going to react, each time they do what upsets us, then they have control over us.

It's when we are in control of our emotions, feelings, and actions; that we start to make positive choices, for our lives.

Frustration

Our *frustration* comes, from expectations we place on others, and situations, consciously or subconsciously.

Are we sure those who frustrate us, have all the information needed, to perform what is expected of them?

OR

Do we blame others, for our lack of communication, in explaining our wants, and needs, and what it will take to complete their jobs?

We expect friends to support us, and employees to do their job. What do we do, when that doesn't happen?
How do we hold them accountable, when expatiations are not met?

Do we ever look at ourselves and ask, what role did we play in this situation? Are we sure everyone understood, what he, or she, was supposed to do? What was, or is, expected of him, or her?

If we have expectations, are they reasonable? We have set a standards, that we expect and we know about, because we thought of it. If we think, others should know the rules just because they are adults, the problem is ours. If we think, others who do not know, or understand, the rules should ask, the problem is ours, again.

If you expect certain behaviors, and actions, out of others, it is our job, to make sure they understand the rules, expectations, and consequences. Only when there is a clear understanding, and the expectations are not met, do we start to become frustrated.

If we continue, to become frustrated, we need to ask ourselves, "Who are we really frustrated with, the other person, or us, for not being clear on our expectations?"

Making & Keeping Friends

The reason dogs have so many *friends*,
is that they wag their tails,
Instead of their tongues.

We lose more *friends*,
By running our mouth,
Than by any other action we do.

If we could engage our brain,
B*efore* we engage our mouths,
things would be,
So much better for us.

How many times has someone told us, they had a problem with something, they were told we said about them?

So many of us hear something, or know something about someone, we believe no one else knows, so we think it's okay to tell our very best friend. What we don't think, is our best friend thinks it is okay to tell their best friend, and it may not be you.

Then the tongue wagging (rumors) starts.

If we could just think, for just one minute, before we talk, we would not get into so much trouble, and would have a lot more friends.

How many times, were we in a little trouble, and would not shut up, and ended up talking ourselves into more trouble.
We were told, if you had only just shut-up, this would have been over a long time ago, and you would not have gotten into so much trouble.

The most destructive action, and hurtful thing, we do a lot, is talk.

Better Future

Your life becomes better,
Only when you become better.

With patience comes time,
and with time comes,
education and experience.

With education and experience,
Comes a better quality of life.

It's a shame we have to wait, until we get older, to recognize time is a great teacher.

If we are honest, and look back on our life, from any age, we will see the things that bothered us in the past, really don't matter anymore, or have lost all meaning.

As we get older, life teaches us, that someone jumping in live is not worth a fight. Someone staring at you is, not looking for a fight.

Unless, we are looking for something to be mad about, or someone to fight with, age and experience teaches us, not to sweat the small stuff, and in the end, it's all small stuff.

With age, education, and experience, we will have a quality of life, we could never imagine early in life.

TRY

As adults, we hear many times, from a wide range of people, of all different ages; "I'll try it, and do the best I can.

I have mediated groups, on anger management and substance abuse, in family therapy, for a number of years and, in working groups, young people in particular, I find many times the words "I'm trying to change, or I'm trying to understand, but I just can't." It leads me, to tell them, that I don't believe they have any commitment to change, or understanding.

If all you are going to do, is try.

History says they are expecting me to tell them it's OK, as long as they are trying. Some of them get very upset, when their trying is not accepted. It is sometimes very hard, for some youth/teens and/or adults, to accept the idea that their parents/guardians may have unconsciously misled them, and taught them to fail.

Some young people work very hard on trying to attempt things and are committed to the idea that everything will be OK, if they only try. As these children grow up, although they believe they try very hard, they may now start getting into trouble, are fired, for not completing what they are trying, or have been asked to do. Many do not understand why, because they have tried, and as a rule they were taught it has always been good enough; but now people are not accepting those who only try.

The following section may help you understand why. In the beginning, we believed, try was good enough, then when it stopped working, why, for some, it is so hard to understand.

Definition: Webster's School Dictionary: **try\tried\ trying:**
1. a: to examine or investigate judicially b; to conduct the trial of;
2. a: to put to test or trial; b: to test the limit or breaking point : STRAIN
(try one's patience) **3.** to melt down and obtain in a pure state: RENDER
(try lard from pork fat) **4.** to make an attempt : ENDEAVOR [from Old
French, " to pick out, sift"].
* **synonym-** ATTEMPT, STRIVE: TRY suggests effort to experiment
made in hope of determining facts, or of testing, or proving something
(tried various occupations);
ATTEMPT suggests a beginning of or venturing upon something and
often implies failure (attempted to break through the enemy lines);
STRIVE implies effort (strive to achieve lasting peace) – try one's hand:
to attempt something for the first time.
Appropriate Use: Try is used when organizations, or individuals, want to
create something new, or take something, that has already been built and
make it do something different.
**In both cases you try it once, and then work on it until it is
complete.**
In our personal life: to create excitement or challenges.
Professional: In the legal system, "How will we try the case?"
Medical: "We need to try something?"
Business: "Let's try and buy that company?"
Management: To employees, "Would you try to see if you can make this
thing better?" or "This tool doesn't do what I want,
so let's try and find a better one."

Personal: "Let's try to climb that, or I'm going to try and redo this, with
fewer parts and in less time."
All of these things are positive, and "try" implies motivation. When used,
in this context, it generates thought, teamwork, and energy.
Inappropriate use: Try may be used, at times, as an excuse for not
completing something.

Personal Use: I tried to do what you asked, but couldn't.
That invention you wanted me to try, I worked on it some, but couldn't
come up with anything, but I did try.
We tried to climb that thing but we didn't make it.
We will try something different next time.
I tried my new this, and that, but it made me so mad, I quit.

Learning to Fail: When we very young, we were told, at one time or Another, by our parents/guardians to try something, whether it is food, a chore, or homework. If we didn't like it, or didn't think we were able to do it, we didn't have to do whatever it was, as long as we tried. With this being told, and validated by our parents, we soon learned, and understood, that it is ok,

if we try and don't succeed (fail), and we understand there are no consequences, or trouble, as a result.

Each time we came back to our parents, and said "I couldn't do it." They would ask, "Did you try?" When you said yes, they in most cases would say "it's okay, at least you tried."

Creates behaviors: If, when you grow up, you do not make the intellectual Transformation, from trying and not completing something being OK, then failure will become acceptable by only trying. It is very easy to understand youth growing up believing, if we are told to try something, or saying we are only going to try, could imply that we might not have to complete it.

Using the word try, when asking people to do things, could be understood we are

OK if is not completed; however, we actually wanted it done in the first place.

If we are told this often enough, we will come to understand, that if we are only told to try something, it really doesn't matter if we complete it, and we may come to a time when we may not even begin. Being taught the behavior try, we learn,

means not having to complete something, or it's OK to fail.

Taking this further, as we grow up and we start to get into trouble, our parents/guardians tell us to at least try, and stay out of trouble. We then get into trouble again and are told, "what did, we tell you last time?"

You say, "I tried but just can't stay out of trouble."

You don't understand why you're trying and not succeeding is no longer accepted.

It was always a good enough excuse in the past, because that is what we were taught. When we keep getting into trouble, or have trouble keeping a marriage working, holding down a job, stopping from drinking/using drugs, we wonder why we have to pay the consequences for our actions, why no one accepts trying any longer. In most cases, we have not learned other ways to deal with things, because our parents/guardians taught us that to try was good enough.

Using Alternative Words: Part of what we teach our children is it's OK to Fail, if you at least try. The meaning kids get growing up, is, it's OK try is to fail. When I hear a lot of kids say, all right, "I'll try it." I know the majority are not going to complete the effort. I believe, subconsciously, they never were going to complete it, in the first place. Many of the kids, use the words try and fail in the same sentence, as if the two words have the same meaning to them. We hear, "I have been in trouble most of my life and try as hard as I can, but I am still in trouble. I am just a failure." 99.

Unless along the way, we receive some awareness, we will use the same word to describe our failed marriage, our inability to stay off drugs/alcohol or keep a job – We try, but we just can't make it work, because try is still our only option.

Whenever we acknowledge, and accept the fact, that we have tried and stopped, in our minds it's final. This is because, most of the time, we were never expected to finish, we could get up from the table, or stop whatever we were doing, except to go back and try again. So rather than use try and

make failure final, I now ask the families and individuals I work with to Replace "try", with "Work on it."

"Work on it" is always in the present tense. It can mean that, although it isn't completed, I haven't finished, or there may not be a time frame for completion. By working on it and not using the word try/tried, when referring to the not-completed task, gives us an opportunity not to feel defeated. Continuing, to work on it, can make us feel that we are still completing something, slow as it may be,

we still feel good, and haven't failed.

If at first you don't succeed, continue to work on it.
If children are not given proper Understanding,
How to use the word TRY,
They may grow up to be failures and
Not understand Why.

Successful

When you become *successful* in life,
You must remember,
That you did not, do it by yourself.

It is a shame, that most of us,
Do not understand,
Until we get much older.

If we could only see, others as helpful,
and not trying to tell us what to do,
We would be much better off.

If you refuse or reject,
Help being offered,
It may not be available,
When you really need it most.

Sometimes, we become so proud of ourselves, for something we managed to accomplish, that we forget all those that helped us.

When we were smaller, and involved in sports, who made sure we got to school every night? We took it for granted, that's what parents do. We never think they organized their evening, around us.

When we are older, and involved in a social clubs, or social activities that takes us out of the house, or away for our family.
How much support does our family give us?
Do we even think about it?

When we put in extra time at work, to earn a promotion?
How many people help us, or sacrifice time, for our goal?

Sometimes, we also don't think about the ones around us, who offer advice and direction. If we get so caught up in ourselves, we may ignore, and reject, some very important information.

No matter what we think, we have been helped, many times during our lives. Successful people recognize that help, and support, often.

Weak vs. Strong

"Giving up, doesn't always mean you are *weak* ...
Sometimes it means, that you are *strong* enough to let go."

Sometimes we beat ourselves up,
Thinking we are *weak*, or quitters,
and keep going even to our detriment.

If you have given it you're all,
It is a weakness to keep going,
in an unhealthy environment.

Having the pride and strength,
To act, and move on, builds integrity,
Makes you stronger in the future,
so not to settle for things,
You do not want to.

It is all well and good to say, "I'm not a quitter." Sometimes, it is not the smartest thing to say. If we add up all the time, we spend on things we are not able to finish, for whatever reason, it could be days, weeks, or even months, look at what it was we were actually trying to do, and in a lot of cases, what we were doing didn't matter at all.

When we start something that ends up, giving us a very hard time, it shows a real maturity to say, "STOP, enough is enough. I have spent enough time on this." It may have cost us a lot of money, or time, or both, but you still have to draw a line.

Having a hobby is one thing, but when it becomes an obsession, are we strong enough to say stop? A lack of fortitude lets us keep going on things we should have stopped doing, a long time ago.

What is this costing me? A question, not many of us really ask.
How much real money, and time, am I taking away from myself, and my family? Has my project, or goal, gotten out of perspective, and become more important than it needs to be?

Do we try and do it all on our own? Do we involve others, who may be affected by the time, and money, we are using?

Message or Messenger

When someone is trying to give you advice,
and you do not want to hear it,
Are you rejecting the **message**?
Or the **messenger**?

Why is it we reject, and at times get mad,
When our parents give us advice,
But we listen to that same advice,
From someone else, who doesn't know us,
Nor has any responsibility for us?

"Why is it, our parents get smarter, the older we get"?
Is a cliché for a reason.

Do we really understand what is going on with us?
When we reject what we know is good advice?
Do we ever ask ourselves, who is giving us advice or direction?
What impact do they have on my life?
We, at times, hear the same advice, over and over.
(We call them lectures) Do we ever ask why is everyone giving me, the same lecture, all the time?
Do we ever question our behavior and actions?
If we are not listening, and continue doing the same thing,
It is no wonder people are giving us the same advice all the time.
If we understood that it is us, that is generating the comments, and advice others are giving us.
Do we really look at the role we play, in our growing and maturing? If we want approval and acceptance from adults,
What are we doing to get that acceptance and approval?

Is it, we reject advice from our parents, because they always watch and listen to us? Is it, they already told us what was going to happen, and it turned out they were right?

Do we hate our parents being right, and loving to prove them wrong? Just because it happened to our parents, or they think they know what is going to happen, why does it have to happen to me?
Why will we listen to friend's parents, someone from church, or an older person we may know? Why is it, all the people we listen to have little, or no authority, or responsibility over us? It may also be because our parents are the ones who will give us consequences.
If after they tell us, not to do something, for the same reason they knew something was going to happen, and now they have been proven right (which makes you mad). Now, you are going to also get consequences, for not listening and breaking a rule.

Are our parents the messenger we don't like, or is it the message?

The Lesson

"The greatest *lesson* in life, is to know,
That even fools are right sometimes."

Winston Churchill

It is important to remember,
That everyone has an idea,
And the ability to figure things out.

Are we fair in our judgment?
About whom we ask to help us?
Do we only pick?
Who we think is smart?
And ignore the rest?

Picking others, who we think will help us with problems, or those who will give us good ideas, when we don't have any, is a serious form of prejudice. It may sound smart to surround yourself with intellectually superior people, but do they have any common sense?

Some do not present themselves very well, and at times, give a less than positive first impression. Just like some of us, who are really very smart, but do not test very well. All that says is that we do not test well, and has *absolutely* no reflection, on how smart we really are.

Listening to others with an open mind, and getting to know them, may at times really surprise you. There are so many out there, who did well in school, or are prolific readers, and are knowledgeable, on a wide range of topics, but are shy and do not engage themselves early, but need to feel comfortable. One of their fears is the fear of embarrassing themselves. They are the ones, who sit at the back, knowing all the answers, but do not have the nerve to speak up.

I find some very interesting, and surprising, people just talking about random subjects.

Given the opportunity, people like to demonstrate their knowledge, and show others of what they are capable.

Listening to children, will really surprise you, on how much they understand, and think about.

Senior citizens also have a lot to say, but like children are dismissed offhandedly. Children are judged, as not having sufficient age and knowledge, to have a real opinion. Seniors are judged, as not having kept up with technology, having too much age, and too little knowledge, about *today's* world to be of any use.

Are we prejudice and judgmental, about groups and individuals, before we get to know them?

Don't Burn Bridges

Don't burn bridges.
You'll be surprised,
How many times,
You have to cross the same river.

After you tell your boss off,
and quit your job out of a moment of anger,
Do you later wish you could get it back?

You say something hurtful, burn that bridge,
Then later realize, you destroyed a great relationship.

We do not have future sight,
So you may never know when you need help,
or a job, from someone you burned in the past.
So, *don't burn bridges.*

There are times in our lives, when someone we thought was a friend really isn't, or they worked for us, and it turns out they lied to us, or stole something from us. After we find out, we say, "I can't wait until that person needs something. They were good friends of mine. I wonder why they did that. I find it really hard to understand. They destroyed a really great friendship."

Not only do we burn bridges, but we find out, it was over something, that really didn't matter at all.

We quit jobs, over what at the time, seems like a principle, and we later find out, it was just our ego. We get offered a job, but they are not paying, what we think we are worth, and we tell them that.
They give the job to someone else, and six months later, we are still looking for a job, and will now take almost any salary.
We go back and ask them, if they still have any vacancies, they say no, but would not hire us anyway, because they know, we do not like the salary. We burned another bridge.

A sign of maturity is, when you can disagree, and part as adults, willing to agree to disagree, continuing to maintain respect for each other.

Cool Off

Give yourself an hour to *cool off*,
Before responding to someone,
Who has provoked you.
If it's something really important,
Give yourself overnight.

There are a lot of people divorced,
dead, or in jail, for acting without thinking,
When stepping back, giving the situation a break,
Without any further action.

How many times, do we look at what we did, or said, yesterday, and ask ourselves, "Why was it so important, that we had to say what we did right then?" Did we really think about what we were saying, or doing? Did we know how much, our words could hurt?

When we say, or do things, when we are angry, or upset, we need to understand, at the time we may not be thinking rationally.
The ones we hurt the most, are the ones closest to us. Our partner and children are sometimes really affected, by what is said about them, or their relationship to us, when we are angry, or when we are under the influence of alcohol, or drugs.

When we are angry, something may seem very important, that in the morning will have no value, or meaning at all. Then, we are told what we said and did. Making us really question why?

That old thing about counting to 10, before you speak out of anger, is a real good thing. The number should be **100**, and **doing it,
Not an option.**

Cooling off, before we put our foot in our mouth, May very well, stop the taste of shit the next day.

Luck

Unsuccessful people say,
Successful people have all the **luck**.
They also say, they have no **luck**,
and never get a break.

Successful people believe in,
Hard work and opportunities,
and opportunities mean hard work.
Successful people do not believe in *luck*.

"I am a great believer in **luck**,
I find the harder I work,
the more of it I have".

Steven Leacock

How many times have we said, or heard said, "Man, if I didn't have bad luck, I wouldn't have any luck at all"?

I guess the question is, "What Role did I play?" in directing myself to be successful. How much do I depend on luck? Hope things go smooth this time?
Did we have one of those days, where not a lot of effort was made to get things done, and still hoped they would get done? Did we hope someone would come by and help us (I was lucky you came by), or just hope, for some reason, whatever we were doing would just go away?

What is it that lets us accept having, or not having, luck, a controlling factor on our happiness? When we have a good day, it has nothing to do with luck. If we look back on our activities, during the day, we will be able to see, a lot of our success was because of our attitude toward the work, and how we approached the day, in general.
When you check the lottery results, and see that your numbers didn't win, you say, "It's lucky I didn't buy a ticket this time".
It has nothing to do with luck; you just didn't buy the ticket.

When we work hard, and have the attitude that goes along with a hard worker, people notice us, and more work comes our way (we were not lucky). When we have a loving wife, and a strong family, we worked to deserve that love and family. We were not lucky. When we are silver haired, and have our children, and grandchildren, around us it was work, and a lot of it.
We were not lucky.

Success and happiness are what come from hard work, and the satisfaction that comes from personal accomplishments, not luck.
Remember, the harder you work, the more luck you will have.

Time Management

Don't ever say, you did not, have enough *time*.
You have exactly, the same number of hours per day,
That were given to:
Helen Keller, Pasteur, Michelangelo,
Mother Teresa, Leonardo da Vinci,
Thomas Jefferson, and Albert Einstein.

What did these people do, that a lot of us don't?
The thing they did, was organizing and managing their *time*,
Not just every now and then,
But on a consistent and regular basis.

How many times, have we said, "There just wasn't enough time to get it done honey, I'll finish it tomorrow?"

We sometimes take on more, than we are physically able to do, in the time allotted, just to make someone else happy.
That person could be your boss, who you are trying to impress, or your wife who you are trying to make proud of you, and impress as well. A lot of the times, we genuinely start out, with a day of work planned and WE screw it up.
When we are asked, if we could do something more, a lot of us really believe we can fit it in somehow, and still get, all the work we needed to get done completed. Not only, do we not end up completing all our work, trying to get it all done (including the new job), our quality of work will suffer as well. We normally do not have a problem, working out how much work we can do, in an allotted time. Our problem, is sticking to the schedule.
We would impress more, if we were honest, and explained we did not have enough time today, but, if you got finished early, or a job was cancelled, you would let them know right away, or they can just leave it, and you will get to it once all the other work is completed.

If others seem, to get more done each day, than we do, maybe we should just ask them how, or maybe just watch them, and see what they are doing different.

If we learn at an early age, to plan and manage our time daily, we would find we are much more productive daily. As we grow up, we will be able to take on bigger, more complicated tasks.

The one thing, we all have in common is the length of the day.
The difference is how we use that time.

Think Ahead

When considering your words and actions,
Take time to *think ahead*,
So you will not have any regrets tomorrow.

Most of us, wanting instant gratifications,
Do not really think,
Past our own satisfaction.
The cost of having what we want now,
May, in the end,
Be more than we can afford to pay.

Think ahead.

When we make promises and break them, for whatever reason,

Do we let someone down?

Why did we make the promise in the first place?

If we meant to keep it, what stopped us?

Making the promise was very important, at the time, and it was made for both people involved. By breaking that promise, are you telling the other person that the promise made, is now not as important to you, as it was when you first made it.

There is a good chance, you are going to not only break the promise, but hurt the other persons feelings as well. This promise may have been, very important to the other person, and they may feel really let down by you, after they put so much trust in you. They made sure, they were going to live up to their end of the promise, and will organize themselves to keep the promise, they made at the same time to you.

Role Model

Oh, we understand what being a *role model* means. Do we as parents, adults, & leaders really appreciate that role?

Our children see, hear, and understand much more than we think they do. When, as parents, we say one thing and do another, our children see, and hear, that's what all parents do.

When as leaders (community, state & federal, church and sports), we talk behind someone's back (no guts to go face to face), we spread rumors, we break the law and get away with it, Do we ever think, what impact our actions have, on the youth/teens & future leaders of our nation?

We, as parents & leaders, have no one to blame when our youth/teens get arrested, or expelled from school, or get fired from their jobs, but ourselves. We set the standard, and the role, our youth will play in the future.
We MUST remember our youth are like sponges, and will absorb whatever they see, and hear, in the environment they are placed in. As they get older, what they absorbed, in their childhood environment, will come out when they become adults. We must never forget anyone can be a parent;
it takes no real skill to make a child.
The skill is to be the guiding light, an appropriate role model.

Parenting is hard work. Any parent, who takes real pride in being a parent, will tell you, if you have the nerve to ask, and want to hear the truth.

Parenting is paying attention, even when you do not want to; dropping off and picking up at all hours; attending **all** parent teacher meetings, and when you see a conflict of dates and times, adjust it, to be at any meeting, that concerns the future of your child/children. If you don't, your child will see that, whatever you choose to do was more important than them. In their still developing minds will believe they are second. That is not what you intended, but it is definitely what they get out of it.

Children do learn how to treat others, talk to others, respect authority, respect other races, respect other religions, respect other classes of people, and generally have an open mind to things they do not understand.
They do learn how to ask questions, and research information, before making a judgment about someone. They also learn that others will have an opinion, that is different from theirs, and that is okay.

What our children also learn is how to be a role model, for those younger than them, and their children in the future.

In being the Role Model we need to be,
with those who look up to, and respect us, is,
"What Role am I Playing, in the future life of my child/children."

I believe, the terms **Parent** and **Role Model,**
should always be used in the same sentence.

Helping Hand

Lending a ***helping hand***,
Should be a joyful thing,
As we all need help at times.
It should not come with a price attached.
When lending a ***helping hand***,
It is normally because someone needed it,
and you feel able to lend a ***helping hand***.

When you offer help to someone in need,
There is no pay-back price on it.
If there is a payback price,
The payback will be,
You both have a good, and honest,
Friend for life.

If someone didn't need help, and you still helped,
like a neighbor or friend, you did it, out of the goodness of your heart.
You cannot ask, or imply later, that they should help you.

If someone asked for your help, and said, they
would pay you back one day, that's okay.
One day in the future, you need some help, and you ask
for their help, they should help you.
After all they do owe you.

When helping others, you are going to want it
paid back later. It is smart, to have any repayment
agreement decided, before any work even starts, because
the person needing help, may not be able, or want,
to pay the amount asked.

How many times, after being helped out, of what seemed
like friendship, did the person that helped you, come back
later and say, "I helped you, now you owe me,"
and now I want (not *need*, but *want*) your help.
This kind of attitude destroys a lot of friendships.

**Please remember, there is no obligation
to be someone's friend.**

www.ingramcontent.com/pod-product-compliance
Lightning Source LLC
Chambersburg PA
CBHW051444280526
45785CB00003B/1418